T0081945

To access audio visit:
www.halleonard.com/mylibrary

Enter Code
1617-1047-5885-3938

Audio Arrangements by Peter Deneff

ISBN 978-1-61780-576-9

HAL•LEONARD®
CORPORATION
7777 W. BLUEMOUND RD. P.O. BOX 13819 MILWAUKEE, WI 53213

Visit Hal Leonard Online at
www.halleonard.com

BACK TO DECEMBER

Words and Music by
TAYLOR SWIFT

Horn

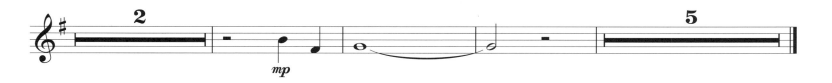

BLANK SPACE

Horn

Words and Music by TAYLOR SWIFT,
MAX MARTIN and SHELLBACK

To Coda ⊕

D.S. al Coda
(take all repeats)

CODA ⊕

mf

f

1.

2.

FIFTEEN

Horn

Words and Music by
TAYLOR SWIFT

I KNEW YOU WERE TROUBLE

Horn

Words and Music by TAYLOR SWİFT, SHELLBACK and MAX MARTIN

9

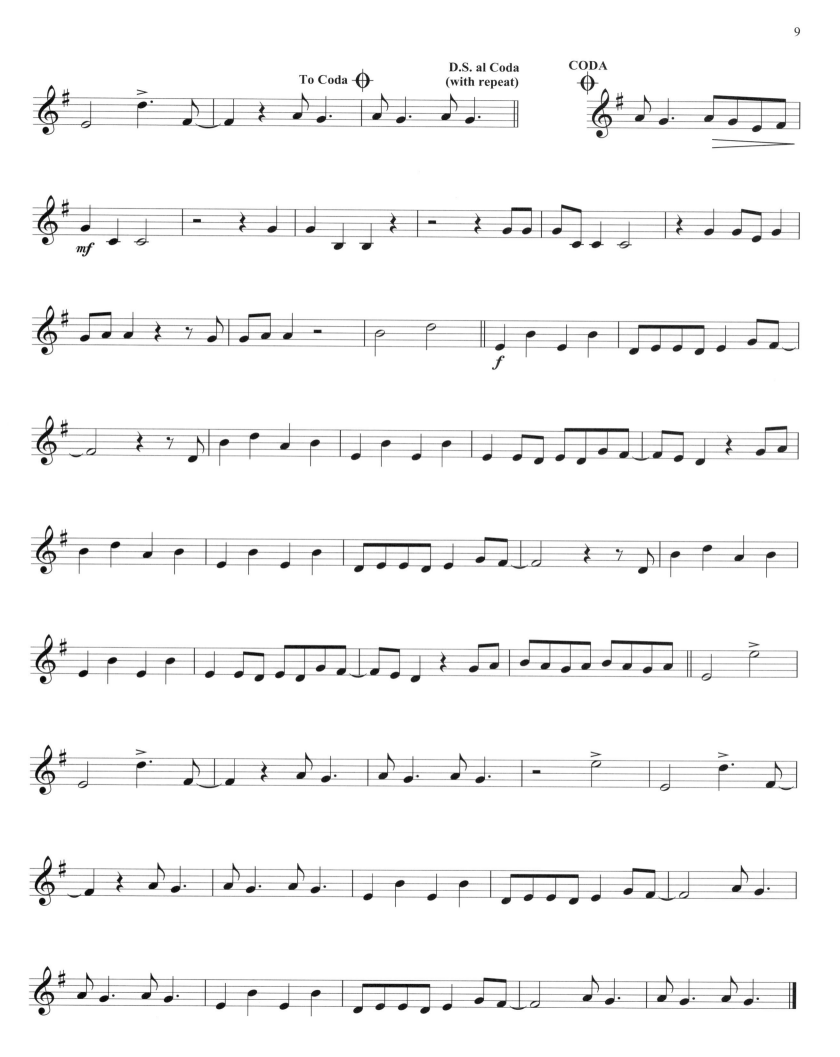

LOVE STORY

Horn

Words and Music by
TAYLOR SWIFT

MEAN

HORN

Words and Music by
TAYLOR SWIFT

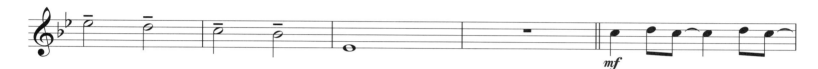

14

OUR SONG

Words and Music by
TAYLOR SWIFT

PICTURE TO BURN

HORN

Words and Music by TAYLOR SWIFT
and LIZ ROSE

17

SHAKE IT OFF

Horn

Words and Music by TAYLOR SWIFT,
MAX MARTIN and SHELLBACK

D.S. al Coda
CODA

SHOULD'VE SAID NO

HORN

Words and Music by
TAYLOR SWIFT

TEARDROPS ON MY GUITAR

Horn

Words and Music by TAYLOR SWIFT
and LIZ ROSE

22

Horn

Words and Music by TAYLOR SWIFT,
SHELLBACK and MAX MARTIN

WE ARE NEVER EVER GETTING BACK TOGETHER

Horn

Words and Music by TAYLOR SWIFT,
SHELLBACK and MAX MARTIN

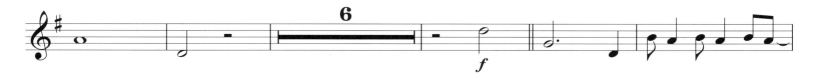

WHITE HORSE

Horn

Words and Music by TAYLOR SWIFT
and LIZ ROSE

YOU BELONG WITH ME

HORN

Words and Music by TAYLOR SWIFT
and LIZ ROSE